GLACIER-WATERTON EXPL[

BY CARL SCHREIER

INTRODUCTION BY A.B. GUTHRIE, JR.

HOMESTEAD PUBLISHING
MOOSE, WYOMING

FOR GOLDIE SCHREIER
mother, teacher

Published by Homestead Publishing
Post Office Box 193, Moose, Wyoming 83012

Acknowledgements
Design by Carl Schreier
Production by Liz Finegan, John Thompson
Editing by Angus Thuermer
Typography by Linda Moyer
Lithography by Paragon Press

Cover photo: St. Mary Lake.
Inside front cover: Sunset from Logan Pass.
Back cover: Mountain goat on Highline trail.
Title page: Eagles on McDonald Creek.
Contents page: Aspen grove.
Introduction: Bracken Fern, Avalanche Creek.

Photo Credits for History Chapter, pages 40-47
Blackfeet Indian Warriors, circa 1900: *Photo by Walter McClintock,*
courtesy National Park Service.
Blackfoot Glacier Crevasse: *Photo by Hileman,*
courtesy National Park Service.
Many Glacier Hotel: *Photo by Hileman, courtesy Mrs. Emily Moke.*
International Boat: *Photo by Hileman, courtesy National Park Service.*

Photography Credits
Bill Conrod - page 23.
All other photographs by the author, Carl Schreier.

CONTENTS

INTRODUCTION

The glories of Glacier National Park and its Canadian twin, Waterton Lakes National Park, are rated differently by different eyes.

Some would cite the grandeur of the mountains, and some the incredible blue of the lakes, some the profusion of flowers; but all would grant that, taken together, they constituted a wild and beautiful world.

My first feeling is for the mountains that rise steep from the plains. From the roads that skirt their high bases one looks down into chasms and sees the floating white of clouds. The effect is of heights and depths and space that set the spirit soaring. The spirit wings free, too, at the sight of azure lakes or the bear grass that blows nearly everywhere.

The sense of adventure and awe is heightened when the visitor sees eagles, or bighorn sheep, or wild goats, or, possibly, a grizzly and her cub.

Unlike Yellowstone these parks offer no freaks of nature—no geyser basins, no boiling springs, no Old Faithful. No freaks, that is, unless one counts immensity as a freak, as it becomes when eyes are dazzled by uplifts and drops and waters that might be called Glimmerglass, like the Glimmerglass of James Fenimore Cooper.

The word for these rewards to sight and soul is glory, or majesty, or grandeur. Over the centuries nature, in travail, has delivered them. They make human concerns unimportant.

A.B. Guthrie, Jr.
Author of The Big Sky
Choteau, Montana

Waterton and Glacier. They are romantic names which are aptly descriptive of a romantic country. It is a place where by-gone days are still frozen in time. And where care-free days still exist.

It is also true mountain country, not in the sense of rolling hills, but massive peaks with barren, windswept summits, and chasms, and vertical cliffs, and glaciated valleys. It is on these cliffs and peaks that pure white mountain goats, tawny bighorn sheep, and silver-tip grizzlies are at home.

This country can also boast of nearly 50 glaciers, 250 lakes, and a road which is truly Going-to-the-Sun. But most importantly it is two nations sharing a national park and their common reverence for wild places.

Take this opportunity to explore the pebbly shore of Lake McDonald, the fern-lined gorge of Avalanche Creek, the alpine meadow of Logan Pass, the trails of Many Glacier, and the international waters of Waterton Lakes. Take this time while winter has loosened its grip. For although the summer is short, the memories are long.

The Going-to-the-Sun Mountain becomes shrouded in wisps of clouds as the first snow storm of the season reaches the mountain country.

WATERTON LAKES

Waterton Lakes National Park is where the mountains rise abruptly from the grassland prairie and where a seven and a half mile lake is shared by two countries. It is also a region rich in cold alpine lakes, glaciated cirques and canyons, and spectacular waterfalls.

But Waterton is also known for its natural history and recreation. Some of Earth's oldest rocks are found here, cut and exposed by glacial ice and water. And the lakes provide the recreationist with sports from windsurfing and boating to fishing and swimming. The mountains are laced with hiking trails from which mountain gazers watch sunsets.

Yet even the picture of Waterton is incomplete without its relics of the past. The Prince of Wales Hotel, built in 1927, stands as a landmark overlooking Waterton Townsite and Waterton Lakes. This Swiss-style seven-storied hotel is exposed to the Waterton Lake winds, and bears their full brunt. But the Prince of

Wales was built to flex with gale-force winds. Wrought iron stays allow the steep pitched roof of the upper floors to sway gently with the wind.

Below the hotel on Waterton Lakes the International boat plies the cold waters on its run between Waterton Townsite and Goat Haunt. The wooden ship still retains its glamour and nautical charm of a by-gone time.

Waterton is also famous for its hiking trails. Here they offer easy strolls along the lake shore and climbs up Mount Cleveland, the highest peak in the Parks.

By far the easiest trail is the Lakeshore Trail, or the International Trail, which extends from the south end of Waterton Townsite nine miles one-way to the end of Waterton Lake at Goat Haunt. A trip can be made as long or as short as desired. The most popular excursion is to take a boat shuttle one way and hike the other.

Another popular hike is short but strenuous. The trail head begins behind the information bureau and climbs three-quarters of a mile through Douglas firs to a windswept limestone ridge, called the Bear's Hump, overlooking Waterton Lakes and Townsite.

The Crypt Lake Trail is reached by taking a boat shuttle across the lake from Waterton Townsite to a small landing where the trail

begins. The five-and-a-half mile trail climbs over 2,000 vertical feet to a small isolated cirque lake along the international boundary.

The Bertha Lake Trail is also a popular hike to an alpine lake. The trail starts with the Lakeshore Trail and branches from it a half mile from the trail head. The three-and-a-half mile trail is fairly steep, but leads through a Douglas fir forest past Lower Bertha Falls, up a hanging canyon to a subalpine forest, past Upper Bertha Falls to a high cirque lake. There is a trail which continues around Bertha Lake (named after an early Waterton resident).

The Carthew Trail is a longer hike extending from Cameron Lake at the end of the Akamina Highway to Waterton Townsite. This 12-mile hike, if started from Cameron Lake, drops nearly 3,700 feet in elevation but several ridges add 2,500 feet of climbing. The trail is famous for its panoramic views, especially of Cameron Lake.

An extended two- to four-day hike begins at Goat Haunt and follows the Continental Divide and ends at Logan Pass. The nearly 25-mile trail leads through alpine country, past the base of Mount Cleveland, through grizzly country, connecting with the Highline Trail and Granite Park Chalet.

There are also many other trails in the Waterton area. It is best to consult with a Park Warden to check on trail conditions, closures, and animal sightings before venturing out.

A land of contrasts. Waterton is a park bordering on the prairie and the Rocky Mountains. Bison (upper left) graze on the rolling grasslands at the base of the mountains, while Cameron Falls (lower left) spills from the mountain canyons.

Waterton Lake (right) is divided by an imaginary boundary separating Canada and the United States, and the two countries share a lake, a national park, and friendship.

MANY GLACIER

Many Glacier is a park in itself. Contained within these mountains and this drainage are glaciated canyons, glaciers and alpine lakes. Many Glacier's own climate forms here among the high mountains and is held by steep canyon walls until it escapes out over the prairie. This valley has its own wildlife population; bighorn sheep run free on high alpine meadows and the grizzly relishes huckleberry patches. This is truly a Shangri-la valley.

Many Glacier is also noted for its wildflowers. Beargrass cover the slopes with its stalked cream-colored heads. The yellow star-shaped stonecrop blooms among the dry talus slopes and blue trumpet-like penstemon flowers nearby. Each flower adds another color to the palette.

The Many Glacier area is shaped like a three-fingered hand. Lake Sherburne extends along the forearm terminating at the palm of the hand at Many Glacier Hotel and Swiftcurrent Lake. The northern finger points to Ptarmigan and Iceberg Lakes. The middle finger points to Red Rock and Bullhead lakes and over the ridge to Swiftcurrent Lookout and Granite Park Chalet. The southern digit extends to Lake Josephine, Grinnell Lake and Glacier. All three of these valleys are broad U-shape glaciated canyons lined with subalpine fir in the lower sections, and open grassy alpine meadows above.

From the Many Glacier Hotel a network of trails leads up each canyon to glaciers, lakes, peaks, lookouts, tunnels, and abandoned mines. One of the most popular hikes is along Lake Josephine to Grinnell Lake and Glacier. It is possible to either walk along the lake shore or take the shuttle boat from Many Glacier Hotel across Swiftcurrent Lake to the head of Lake Josephine. From there the trail divides. An easy one mile hike along the bottom of the canyon leads to Grinnell Lake, a small alpine lake at the base of a cliff called Angel Wing. The steep trail leads to Grinnel Glacier with an elevation gain of 1,500 feet in two-and-a-half miles. At its end is a spectacular view of Grinnel and Salamander glaciers. They were once a single glacier, but warming trends have melted them apart. Grinnell Glacier is considered to be the largest glacier in the Park.

A short easy hike begins at the Swiftcurrent Inn passing through aspen and subalpine firs to Red Rock Lake, and after one-and-a-half miles reaches Red Rock Falls. The trail continues and climbs to Swiftcurrent Pass to the McDonald Valley.

Another popular hike is to Iceberg Lake and Ptarmigan Falls, Lake and Tunnel. Iceberg Lake is an easy going four-mile hike beginning at Swiftcurrent Inn and leading to a cirque lake surrounded by sheer cliffs. Large ice blocks are common on the lake throughout the summer, and it receives its name from these. Ptarmigan Falls is along the same trail to Iceberg Lake, and the trail branches there to the lake and tunnel. From the falls it is another one-and-a-half miles to the lake, a small alpine lake cold and refreshing for a mid-summer swim. The man-made tunnel is above the lake and pierces an arête (a glacier-formed wall of rock) and the trail continues through to Elizabeth Lake and the Belly River area.

The Cracker Lake hike from Many Glacier Hotel leads to an abandoned mining operation at a small turquoise-blue alpine lake surrounded by cliffs. There is an elevation gain of over 1,000 feet along this six-mile hike.

Trails through the Many Glacier-Swiftcurrent Valley (right) lead to glaciers, abandoned mines, waterfalls, tunnels, and cirque lakes, like Ptarmigan Lake (left).

LOGAN PASS

Logan Pass is Going-to-the-Sun country. It is a place where the Going-to-the-Sun Road peaks on its journey from Lake McDonald to St. Mary. It is a land of snow and ice in winter, and a land of alpine meadows carpeted with wildflowers during the summer. The Continental Divide snakes along here too, following the knife-like ridge of the Garden Wall.

After several weeks of snow removal, the Going-to-the-Sun Road is usually open by mid-June. Snow fields cling to avalanche slopes through most of July, and remnant snow patches remain on top of the 6,649 foot pass. By August the remaining snow has a pinkish tinge to it as algae filaments grow upon the surface, producing "watermelon snow."

Mountain goats wander along the trails and greet hikers to their mountain domain. Pikas and hoary marmots scramble among the rocks, and bighorn sheep graze on the steep mountain slopes, while golden eagles soar among the peaks.

Nearly 800 miles of trails wander among the peaks in Waterton-Glacier, and Logan Pass is the crossroad for many of the best trails. Some follow the crest of the Continental Divide, while others lead to glaciated lakes and mountain peaks.

Boardwalks which lead from the visitor center across the alpine meadows protect the fragile alpine plant life from trampling and erosion. The boardwalk crosses an alpine meadow filled with buttercups, glacier lilies and Indian paint-

brush, and past mountain goats which greet hikers on the trail to Hidden Lake. The one-and-a-half mile hike is a steady, but gradual climb to the overlook of Hidden Lake, and it is one of the best and most likely short hikes to encounter mountain goats.

The Highline Trail to the south of Logan Pass follows the Garden Wall nearly seven miles to Granite Park Chalet. The trail provides a spectacular view of the McDonald Valley and alpine country. The trail is slightly up and down, but there is no change in elevation from Logan Pass to Granite Park Chalet—a back-country hotel providing lodging and meals for guests arriving by foot or horse. The trail continues, eventually ending at Goat Haunt or Waterton Townsite. But there are short diversions to Swiftcurrent Lookout and Grinnel Glacier overlook from the chalet. The trail across Swiftcurrent Pass to Many Glacier Valley

branches from the pass and climbs over 1700 feet and two-and-a-half miles from the chalet, and provides the best view of the entire Waterton-Glacier country. Another short, but steep trail from the chalet branches from the Highline Trail toward Logan Pass and climbs 1,000 feet and one-and-a-half miles from the chalet. The most popular route to return to the Going-to-the-Sun Road is by descending over 2,000 feet over four miles from the chalet to the 'loop' in the road. The Granite Park-Logan Pass country is famous for its grizzly bears. Hikers should remain alert, and make their presence known to give bears ample time to escape.

Mount Reynolds (far right) dominates the skyline above Logan Pass, but any view from Logan Pass (right) is spectacular.

LAKE McDONALD

For the young, or the young at heart, Lake McDonald was made for you. The flat, water-worn pebbles lining the shore of Lake McDonald are ideal for skipping across the placid surface of the lake, and the shallow shore beckons all to wade in its cold waters on a hot summer day. Fishermen troll the lake in the cool misty mornings in hopes of catching cutthroat, bull, or lake trout along the nearly 10 mile lake.

The habitat is different in the McDonald Valley. Lodgepole pine, interspersed with western larch—conifers which lose their needles each fall—cover the slopes. While in the lower valley western red cedar, western hemlock, and Pacific yew are at their eastern limits, and are not found east beyond the McDonald Valley. It is a valley of contrasts and rarities.

McDonald Valley is also known for its salmon and eagle migration. Kokanee salmon begin returning from Flathead Lake, after spending four years in the lake, to their hatching site to spawn. The bald eagles congregate here to feed on the helpless fish in McDonald Creek at Apgar. During the first part of November the bald eagles can number more than 600 along a two mile stretch of the river.

The hikes which originate from the McDonald Valley enter a variety of habitats from fern-lined canyons, to cirque lakes, to fire-lookouts, and to a backcountry chalet.

The Trail of the Cedars to Avalanche Gorge is one of the most popular short hikes in the Park. Massive red cedars and black cottonwoods shelter this narrow canyon, and they have created an environment suitable for fairies and nymphs. The quarter of a mile trail begins at the Avalanche Creek Campground, north of Lake McDonald, and wanders beneath the cedars through ferns, yew, hemlock, and Rocky Mountain maples terminating at the cascade of Avalanche Gorge. The trail continues from there two miles to Avalanche Lake, a cirque lake. It is a fairly easy trail and bears also frequent this area.

The trail to Apgar Lookout climbs over 1500 feet and provides a panoramic view of the McDonald Valley and the Flathead River. A road leads from the West Glacier entrance station to Quarter Circle Bridge and the trail head. From there the trail climbs steeply through lodgepole pines for three-and-a-half miles, to an abandoned fire-lookout station.

Another lookout is perched on Mount Brown near Lake McDonald Lodge. The trail head begins across from the Lodge and leads to Mount Brown and Sperry Chalet and Sperry Glacier. The hike is only five-and-a-half miles long, but it has the greatest elevation change of any trail in the Parks with nearly 4,000 feet of climbing. The view, however, makes up for the long strenuous hike, providing a vantage point overlooking the entire McDonald Valley. And the changes in vegetation provide a study in botany.

From the same trail head as Mount Brown another trail branches from there and climbs nearly 3,000 feet over six miles to Sperry Chalet, a backcountry chalet accessible by foot or horse only and provides lodging and meals to backcountry patrons. A trail continues to climb one mile to a pass and overlooks Sperry Glacier, one of the largest glaciers in the Park.

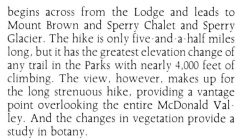

Lake McDonald and the McDonald Valley (right) resembles a fjord from the Highline Trail. McDonald Valley is unique for its vegetation where giant western red cedars dominate Avalanche Gorge and the Trail of the Cedars (left).

Glacial melt water has carved through bedrock creating Avalanche Gorge (left), where the mist and spray of the cascading water has helped establish western hemlocks, bracken ferns, Pacific yew, and western red cedars.

The early morning mist clings to the lake as fishermen troll Lake McDonald (right) in the hope of catching a breakfast trout.

THE YEAR OF THE GRIZZLY

The wind carries the cold, fresh scent of glaciers, and the mountains climb more than a half mile above and descend a half mile below this mountain saddle. Four of us huddle on the barren, windswept Stoney Indian Pass eating our lunch of crackers, cheese, and sardines. It is silent. Only an occasional gust of wind whispers through the stunted subalpine firs just below the summit of the pass.

An audible snap, the breaking of a twig, issues from the stunted undergrowth. At this elevation and habitat the noise could only be caused by one of two animals I thought; a mountain goat or a grizzly.

The crackers were again making their rounds and the conversation resumed, but my attention continued with the thicket. And just when my thoughts were turning to the chilling weather a lanky, dark-haired grizzly stepped from the undergrowth 20 paces away. We met, man and bear, predator and predator,

Summer is the season for wildlife and wildflowers. Bighorn sheep along the Garden Wall have moved to higher summer pastures to avoid the heat and flies of lower elevations. By July the green tussock 'grass' will shoot up stalks bearing clusters of cream colored flowers called beargrass.

unemcumbered by zoo bars or the windshield of a car.

Barry Lopez, author *Of Wolves and Men*, was once asked what he would do if he met a grizzly on a trail. He replied, "I would meet the grizzly with how I lived my life." And I too met the grizzly with how I lived my life. My encounter was of curiosity (and we know what curiosity did to the cat). We both stood upright. I made one step closer and observed his dark coat, nearly black, with golden guardhairs. While he stood nose in the air searching for scents, probably from the sardine tin near my feet, I consciously surveyed a plan for escape. The trees were too short, the trail too steep and winding, the cliff above the pass too rocky and slow.

Not only did I meet this grizzly with my past, my experience, my knowledge, but I met him with his past, experience and knowledge. What of his past? Has he had encounters with the neat and orderly world we have designed for nature? Has he found the sheepman's stockade and the scorn of his rifle? Has he discovered a camper's cooler full of oranges, hot dogs, aluminum foil, and beef stew?

His glare and muzzle suddenly moved to the side, my indication he poses no threat. He turns and runs over the pass to the shelter of the

undergrowth while glancing occasionally to his side, at us. This is his home, we are the intruders, yet it is the grizzly who leaves first.

The mountains are the last refuge for the grizzly. The grizzlies which once inhabited the plains are now extinct and only a remnant population remains in the northern Rocky Mountains. It is here in Waterton-Glacier that the grizzly can live throughout the year in its ancestral ways.

The seasons are true and distinct and extreme. It is the interaction of weather, environment, and all living things that compose the grizzlies' home, and by following the grizzly through the year it is possible to become acquainted with the nature, the beauty, the harshness, the gentleness of his mountain home—Waterton-Glacier.

WINTER

From the plains the mountains are light blue and stark. The winds blow and the snow drifts in the coulees. The peaks are windblown and a plume of snow flows from their summits. If it is an extremely cold and harsh winter Waterton Lakes and Lake McDonald will freeze over, becoming a field of white.

The massive track of a grizzly (right) is left along the Highline Trail in the receding snow-line of June. By late November the grizzly, in their winter coat, (left) searches for an appropriate denning site near tree line.

Temperatures can drop below fifty below, Fahrenheit in January and February, and the wind can increase that coldness. Yet Chinook winds can blow from the north, warming and thawing the frozen land. Winter is also known for extreme changes and the greatest temperature change ever recorded in a day happened east of Waterton-Glacier at Browning, Montana on January 23, 1916. On that day the temperature changed 100 degrees, a drop from 44 to 56 below.

Winter is a world draped in white. If an animal does not adapt to the whiteness it becomes prey to those who do. The weasel whose summer brown pelage is shed for a coat of white (except for the black-tipped tail) becomes an ermine tunneling through the snow in search of voles and pocket gophers. The white-tailed ptarmigan also turns white. The mottled brown coat is molted in the fall to a pure white, while the bird still retains its black eyes and bill. This camouflage enables them to remain in the open without detection, and when a snow storm passes the birds wait the storm out by becoming buried in the powder. After the storm passes the birds emerge from their burial, and with their slow strut they plow and tunnel through the freshly fallen snow.

The mountain goats, too, are the color of winter. Their free roaming summer range becomes restricted to windswept ridges and southern exposures where they nibble at lichens and cured alpine grasses and sedges.

The Columbia ground squirrel is nestled ten feet under the snow and another five feet under ground in its burrow along the Continental Divide. They are true hibernators. The fat stored over the short alpine summer sustains them until the increasing daylight and warmer temperatures induce them to emerge. During the long cold winter months their body temperature will drop to just a few degrees above freezing, their heart rate drops to only a few beats per minute, and their kidneys con-

centrate urine. Their sleep is so sound that if they are disturbed it takes several days before they awake.

The grizzly bear is slumbering inside its den at this time of year. Its heart rate and body temperature drop to conserve stored energy—fat. But the slow-down is not as drastic as the Columbia ground squirrel's. The grizzly is a winter sleeper and it can be aroused in a matter of minutes if it is disturbed.

The cubs are born during this hostile climate in the warmth and safety of the den. At birth the cubs weigh nearly one pound, and one or two cubs are most common. From their birth until they emerge from the den in the spring they suckle their mothers rich milk and gain nearly 20 pounds.

APRIL-MAY

By May the grizzlies emerge from their dens. Their digestive system slowly readapts to their omnivorous diet as they search for winter-killed elk and bighorn sheep. Their emergence is the first indication of spring and warmer weather.

Inclement weather is common as the days become progressively warmer. Rain falls in the lower valleys while more snow accumulates among the peaks, and the snow line fluctuates with each passing storm. But the increasing daylight signals plants and animals of the approaching summer.

Along with the emergence of the grizzly from its den comes the sprouting of the first plants. Bright yellow buttercups push through the receding snow bank and follow the retreating snow line, blooming as late as July in the alpine regions. Glacier lilies also bloom among them.

The bison in Waterton begin dropping their calves on the greening hillsides. Rust-colored calves run beside their mother, and their bellies begin to extend after the long, lean winter. The elk, too, have dropped their calves in

lower elevation meadows, and the calves follow their mothers as they move to higher summer pastures.

JUNE

Unpredictable weather continues through June, but the rains bring a profusion of wildflowers as blue camas bloom on the plains east of Glacier. Beargrass shoot up three- to four-foot stalks which support clusters of cream-colored flowers. And the trees—aspen, black cottonwood, paper birch, and western larch—leaf out in a bright display of green.

The mountain goats are finding isolated ledges where the young 'kid' goats are born. Shortly after their birth they stand upon wobbly legs and slowly follow their mother. Within a few days they run along the uphill side of their mother, and if they slip they fall against their mother's side instead of tumbling down the mountain. The older goats begin shedding their winter coat for a shorter, cooler summer coat. Patches of hair begin shedding on their head and neck and by July the last remnant of the old winter coat is all that remains on their rump.

Bighorn sheep remain in small separate bands of males and females. The rams follow the retreating snowline and spend summer in higher pastures while the ewes remain at a lower elevation to raise their young.

Other animals are appearing in June. The Columbia ground squirrels are seeing daylight for the first time after being born weeks before with closed eyes and hairless bodies. Ptarmigan chicks are hatching from faintly spotted eggs laid in a hollowed spot on the barren ground, and their parents are molting to their brown cryptic summer plumage.

Waterton-Glacier becomes locked-up in snow and ice during the winter, and temperatures can drop to 50 below with arctic-like winds.

Beargrass blossoms (right), a member of the lily family with thin linear leaves, are one of the first indicators of the approaching alpine summer when it begins to bloom in June. Mountain goats (far right) with their thin summer coats indicate the warm weather of July. By August the remaining snow on Logan Pass (lower center) turns pink as algae grows on the surface, producing 'watermelon snow.' And by September Indian summer brings a second, warm, short season to the alpine country when grouse (upper center) strut before moving to lower elevations with the coming winter.

In June the daylight hours increase, contrasting with the long, dark midwinter days. At this latitude the summer daylight extends from five in the morning until nearly eleven at night. The longer daylight hours begin melting snowbanks and snowfields and, depending on the severity of the winter, the snowplows and blowers begin working on the Going-to-the-Sun Road during the first half of this month. The road is usually open by the middle of June following several weeks of work.

By June the grizzly has been out of its den for over a month. Its diet becomes more varied and includes glacier lily bulbs, yellowbell corms, and green grass as well as carrion. They are slowly beginning to replenish their stored fat for the next winter. Their old 'grizzled' coat begins to shed for a thinner, cooler summer coat as the heat of July and August approaches.

JULY-AUGUST

The grizzly now wanders in the higher alpine country, searching the avalanche slopes for bulbs of alpine flowers, the burrow of Columbia ground squirrels and carpenter ants under a rotting log. All of these are extracted with powerful front legs and long hooked claws. By August the grizzlies' favorite food is ripening. Sweet purple huckleberries and leaves are stripped from the bushes as they feast during a three-week period.

The alpine trails relinquish the last of the winter's snow, and the alpine meadows are brilliant with flowers. Wildflowers which bloomed during May and June in the lower valleys are now displaying in the alpine meadows. Fields of glacier lilies, hillsides of beargrass, American bistort, and Indian paintbrush add their colors of yellow, white, and red.

Animal life now flourishes in the high country. Animals which wintered in the low country have now migrated to spend summer on the lush green alpine medaows. Mule deer,

bighorn sheep, Clark's nutcrackers, chickadees, water pipits, and gray-crowned rosy finches are now at home in the alpine country.

Mountain goats also move to more inaccessible reaches of the summits and rocky ledges. They have adapted to a winter environment and the heat of July and August sends them searching for snowfields to lie upon while they pant and cool themselves. Mountain goats also have a craving for salt, and they travel to natural mineral licks to satisfy their urge. At Walton, the southern boundary of Glacier, goats travel down the steep embankment of the Middle Fork of the Flathead River to lick the natural minerals there. In the high alpine country a goat's salt craving is apparent when it approaches hikers to lick the perspiration from their forearms.

In the alpine zone the rocks appear to move as hoary marmots and pikas run from rock to rock. The hoary marmot, ranging in color from a light smoky tan to dark brown and black, whistles sharply from its vantage point upon a prominent rock if an intruder wanders too closely. Some call them 'land beavers' because of their resemblance to beavers, but their dry open alpine country does not resemble the habitat of the true beaver.

The pika, closely related to the rabbit, resembles a cross between a rabbit and a mouse. They have the tail of a rabbit and the ears of a mouse, and they are about halfway between the size of the two animals. Pikas are the color of the rocks, and except for their 'pee-ee' call they go unnoticed. Unlike the marmot, who hibernates on stored fat during the winter, the pika harvests grasses and forbs and dries them on rocks during the summer and stuffs its 'haystack' under rocks for use through the winter. Their tunnel system under the snow and rocks lead to separate 'haystacks,' latrines, and sleeping areas.

The alpine areas may be receiving summer in full glory, but in the lower valleys spring and summer is past its prime. Migrant birds have

begun to leave and grasses and forbs begin to cure and turn brown. The soil and duff dries because of lack of rain and the forest becomes kindling for a fire. Lightning-strike fires occur during a dry August but this is not destruction, it is renewal. Fires are not alien to a forest; they have been going on for millions of years and a healthy forest is dependent upon them. In this region, before man, fires burned an area nearly every twelve years, cleaning the duff, brush, and undergrowth, recycling the nutrients, while the smoke acted as a natural insecticide. Western larch and Douglas firs have evolved a thick corky bark around their bases to insulate themselves from fire. However with our interference we have allowed duff and downed timber to pile up. Once a fire sweeps through an over protected forest the fire is hotter and flares into the upper canopy causing more destruction than natural periodic fires of the past.

SEPTEMBER

The grasses have cured, and summer has ended. Labor Day marks the end of summer, and usually by the first or second week of September the first of the winter storms begin. Snowline temporarily moves down the mountain, frosting the rocky peaks and trees to just below timberline. Meantime in the valleys the low-hanging clouds drizzle rain. But this is only temporary. By the last half of September Indian Summer has begun with its hot days and cold nights. It is the second summer of the high

Bald eagles are attracted to McDonald Creek during their migration south to winter in warmer climates. Kokanee salmon, a non-native landlocked salmon, also migrate to McDonald Creek to spawn in the stream and die, ending their four year life cycle. For nearly six weeks, beginning in early October, eagles stop here to rest and feed upon the helpless fish.

country. Bunchgrasses resprout from their seemingly dead bases. Some even flower again during this short warm period. But winter weather is approaching, and the Indian Summer can end suddenly at any time.

With the end of September comes the fall colors. Aspen and black cottonwood begin with their subdued yellows and oranges. Then the flaming orange of paper birch adds its brilliance to the upper canopy. The understory changed color earlier in September when huckleberry and red osier dogwood turned to red, Rocky Mountain maple, thimbleberry and Devil's club to yellow, and mountain ash to orange. And after the display is complete and the wind has stripped the deciduous trees of their leaves, western larch, a conifer which loses its needles, turns yellow-green then bright yellow forming a mosaic against the wooded mountainside.

The grizzlies by now have added extra weight, but they continue to search for food. However most of their food sources have disappeared. The Columbia ground squirrels are gone. They spent the first week or two of September fasting to clean their digestive system in preparation for their winter sleep, and by mid-September their burrow entrances are sealed. The grizzly sniffs at these sealed entrances, knowing there is a possible dinner underneath, but its attempt at excavation by removing several cubic feet of earth proves futile.

OCTOBER-NOVEMBER

A coldness is prevalent in the air, and each day winter weather threatens. The grizzlies have replaced their thin summer coats with thick, bulky ones, making them roly-poly looking in preparation for the winter. By November they are searching for denning sites. They search the avalanche slopes near timberline for appropriate dens. They wander near the dens, until the next heavy snowfall

seals them in. If it is a mild winter they will periodically awaken from their winter sleep and roam about, returning to their den after a day or two.

The goats have prepared for the coming winter by moving to their winter range. Their coats have thickened, and they too, do not resemble their sleek summer selves. The bighorn sheep are also moving down to their winter range after mating season. The rams have performed their head-on collisions, butting each other with tremendous force to impress a potential harem. But the two sexes winter in different areas after this ritual.

Winter has finally arrived to the high country, but the valleys are a few weeks behind. In the McDonald Valley kokanee salmon, landlocked salmon introduced to Flathead Lake in 1916, have begun their migration to Lake McDonald to spawn. The adults were also hatched here four years earlier, and they are now returning to leave their progeny before their own lives pass. During their 50-mile journey the salmon do not eat, and their own digestive system serves as stored nutrition. The male salmon undergo metamorphosis, becoming reddish and larger with a jutting hooked jaw. The salmon congregate between the outlet of Lake McDonald, at Apgar, and the confluence with the Middle Fork of the Flathead River, along the two mile stretch of McDonald Creek, and most spawning occurs near the Apgar bridge.

The salmon attract other animals who feed upon them. Black bears and grizzlies wander along the pebbly shore to feed upon dead or stranded fish. But the most famous visitor to feed upon the salmon is the bald eagle. They congregate here from as far as Alaska and the upper regions of Canada during their migration south. Eagles begin arriving in October. The young ones come first. By the first week in November the eagles number nearly 600, and they line the shore and weigh the trees down along McDonald Creek.

The beginning of winter can be marked by the closing of the Going-to-the-Sun Road. It is kept open until the first major storm covers Logan Pass with heavy snow. Then the gate near the 'loop' is closed until June. With this the year is complete and the cycle begins again.

By late fall winter weather becomes unpredictable along the Garden Wall as the snowline moves down the mountain. Animals preparing for winter have the choice of migrating, hibernating or adapting to the harsh environment.

GLACIERS
OF WATER AND ICE

A cool breeze begins to blow gently from the upper reaches of the St. Mary Valley. It is chilled by glacial ice and funneled by steep valley walls. The barometric pressure falls. The wind reaches gale force at the constriction of St. Mary Lake where the mountains and the Lewis Overthrust Fault end and the plains begin. The cobalt-blue water of St. Mary Lake is whipped into a froth as whitecaps move with the wind.

The sky to the west, over the mountains, darkens as a shapeless nimbostratus cloud develops. Gray-blue streaks of rain move down slope, across rocky ridges and timbered gullies, to the lake where rain drops cause the surface to pulsate. The advancing storm moves along the length of the lake and lessens in intensity at the constriction. From there the cloud dissipates as remnants vanish over the prairie.

The mountains create this; their own weather. The eastern-front valleys, like St. Mary, Two Medicine, Swiftcurrent and Waterton are famous for their fierce winds. Twisted forms of exposed trees testify to gale-force winds. The eastern slope of the Continental Divide receives nearly the same amount of precipitation as the western slope, yet the eastern slope is drier and the vegetation is unlike its lush western counterpart. The mountain weather is partially responsible for this, with its drying winds and absence of cloud cover exposing the eastern slope to sun.

While the mountains influence the climate of the McDonald Valley, they also create microclimates within the range—sheltered communities of plants and animals dependent on the specific patterns of high country weather. Avalanche Creek is an example of this. The sheltered pocket of this canyon has helped giant western red cedars, western hemlocks and black cottonwoods grow. They in turn have helped establish Pacific yew, goats-beard lichen and bracken ferns. This is a climax or mature forest, undisturbed for over 150 years. It is possible to view what this area may have looked like in its youth.

Several fires in the past have swept through similar forests causing the maturation cycle to begin again. In 1967 a lightning-strike fire burned below the Garden Wall in the upper McDonald Valley. That young 'forest' is now composed of beargrass and small shrubs of mountain alder, mountain maple and devil's club. Another forest burned in 1929 in the lower McDonald Valley, near Apgar. Today it is more mature than the upper McDonald Valley fire. Western paper birch, small black cottonwoods, shrub-size cedars and bush-size hemlocks now dominate this semi-moist site.

The climate here in Waterton-Glacier is ever changing. Even a forest fire can change a moist microclimate into a drier site. These are all small climatic changes we can observe in our lifetime. Just as we can find the clues to the changes in a forest, it is possible to find the clues to the changes in the geologic past.

When the Lewis and Clark Expedition explored the upper drainage of the Missouri River they discovered the first clue to Waterton-Glacier's geologic past. Lewis, in his journal, described a river flowing into the Missouri, near the present Fork Peck Reservoir in eastern Montana. His journal states, "the water of this river possesses a peculiar whiteness, being about the colour of a cup of tea with the admixture of a tablespoon full of milk. From the colour of its water we called it Milk river."

The Milk River begins in Glacier National Park where its headwaters are fed by glacial melt. In his journal Lewis actually described rock flour—rock ground so fine by glaciers it becomes suspended in water. Little was known about glaciers, or even that they existed in North America, during Lewis and Clark's time.

Glacier National Park was not named for the glaciers which now occupy isolated niches in the interior. Even though some speculate there are nearly 50 glaciers in the Parks, most are small and border on being called snowfields. Instead, Glacier Park was named for the glacial carving left by the ice ages.

During the past three million years four major ice ages occurred in North America. Each succeeding ice age destroyed the evidence of earlier glaciation. The present landscape was formed during the last ice age in the Pleistocene Epoch which ended 10,000 years ago. The glaciers of the Pleistocene Epoch covered most of the Parks, except for the highest peaks. The plains to the east were even more impressive as massive continental glaciers flowed south.

The glaciers which remain are smaller versions of the great Pleistocene glaciers which formed the topography for which Waterton-Glacier is famous. Glaciers like Blackfoot, Jackson, Sperry, Pumpelly, Grinnell, Kintla, and Agassiz are the best known in the Park. Since the turn-of-the-century, when these glaciers were surveyed and measured, most have dwindled to less than half their size. But after a strenuous hike to any of these remote glaciers their appearance and size is still impressive.

A glacier is a moving stream of ice. The structure of glacial ice is unlike refrigerator ice cubes, it is denser with less air, and because of its mass it becomes plastic-like when it moves. Glacial ice is also not quick-frozen like the surface of a winter pond, instead it is the accumulation of winter snow which changes to a crystalline structure under pressure. As the layers accumulate the air and impurities are

forced out leaving dense ice at the bottom. The denseness of the ice causes the bottom to become plastic, or pliable. The glacial ice needs to be over 100 feet thick and, depending on the temperature and the gradient of the slope, it can flow between a few feet to several hundred feet annually. Grinnell Glacier, one of the largest, moves between 30-50 feet a year.

These rivers of ice also carry out the three-fold glacial process; erosion, transportation, and deposition. The head of a glacier breaks up bedrock by freezing it, and the movement of the glacier frees the rock from the stratum. The rock then becomes incorporated into the ice and is carried along. The continued quarrying of the bedrock produces an amphitheater-like bowl, or cirque, with steep, high walls. When two glaciers in adjacent valleys carve at

a rock wall they reduce the wall to a ridge or a steep, narrow blade of rock with a ragged crest called an arête. Grinnell Glacier has helped form an arête along the Garden Wall.

The rocks which were plucked at the cirque and incorporated into the ice are scoured along the bedrock as the glacier flows. The friction of the two rocks produces deep striations, or glacial grooves in the bedrock. The rock within the glacier is pulverized to a fine rock flour. Glaciers follow the topography of previous stream beds, but their carving and scouring broadens and straightens those valleys into a broad U-shape. Irregularities in the underlying bedrock produce crevasses in the glacier. Although the glacier moves, the surface cracks remain at a fixed position, indicating that the glacier is flowing over a ridge of bedrock.

The Pleistocene glaciers were massive compared to Waterton-Glacier's remnant forms. Those ancient glaciers could actually be called frozen rivers with tributary glaciers flowing into them. Many of the valleys, like Waterton, St. Mary, and McDonald, were nearly full to the brim with flowing ice. Tributaries, or side canyons, flowed into the major valley glacier. These smaller glaciers did not gouge the side canyons as deeply as the main glacier, and after the glaciers disappeared the side canyons were left suspended higher than the valley. Hanging canyons are common in this country, and many have waterfalls where they abruptly drop off to meet the valley.

Eventually a glacier reaches a point where the ice begins to melt. If it is a stable glacier the foot will remain constant year after year. For this to happen more snow must fall during the winter than melts during the summer. However, the glaciers here have been receding over the past century, since recorded measurements, and may have completely vanished.

The foot, or terminus, of a glacier is the end of the conveyor belt for glacier-carried rock.

A glacier in motion. Grinnell Glacier (right) is a moving stream of ice collecting rock and snow along its slow moving journey. Grinnell Glacier moves about 30-40 feet per year, but warming trends are reducing the size and movement each year.

Glacial ice (left) is denser than 'quick frozen' water. Pressure has squeezed the air and impurities out of glacial ice forming a nearly rock-hard ice which scours and scrapes as it flows.

The farthest advance of a glacier is marked by a berm of unconsolidated sand, gravel and cobbles called a terminal moraine. A terminal moraine is not formed by bulldozer action, as might be believed. Instead it is a remnant of melted glacial ice. The Pleistocene moraines today appear as hummocky, tree-covered ridges, and many of the moraines hold lakes behind them. However St. Mary Lake was not formed by a moraine, but by alluvial material deposited by a stream. And the Prince of Wales Hotel does not sit upon a moraine, but upon a ridge of Altyn-Waterton Limestone overridden and polished by glaciers.

Below the moraine the glacial run-off forms an expansive outwash plain. The water deposits silts, sands, and gravels. Lenses of pure, uniform sand are laid down next to similar depositions of smooth, rounded gravel. The water-laid deposits also form nearly perfect layers of alternating silt, sand and gravel.

Outwash plains are generally flat and gradually sloping. But occasionally large chunks of ice become buried by outwash debris. As the ice slowly melts a depression is formed, which sometimes fills with water, forming a kettle lake. North of Waterton Townsite, at the buffalo paddocks, the grassland topography is hummocky with knolls and depressions. This is the outwash plain from the Pleistocene glaciers in Waterton, Cameron, and Blakiston valleys.

And so the topography of Waterton-Glacier has been formed by the carving and polishing action of the ancient Pleistocene glaciers. If the glaciers had not been here the peaks would not have their sharp 'Matterhorns,' or the valleys would not be as straight and steep-walled. Instead the topography would have been smooth and rounded, with only water, not ice, playing the major role in erosion.

The carving by Pleistocene glaciers is only half of the clues to Waterton-Glacier's geologic past. The other clues lie within the rocks themselves—ancient sedimentary rocks dating back to over one billion years ago. It was during that time that shallow seas inundated most of the Pacific Northwest and western Canada. An alternating wet and dry environment and a changing atmosphere continued until nearly 600 million years ago depositing silt, mud, and sand in uniform layers.

Fossils are rare in these sedimentary layers. Even though animal forms did exist they may have been soft-bodied and their remains did not fossilize. However stromatolites, a primitive form of blue-green algae which formed colonial mounds in the intertidal zone, have

left fossil impressions of their existence. These fossils are not the remains of their algae tissue. Rather, as the plants grew the release of carbon dioxide caused the surrounding water to become alkaline which formed a crust of calcium carbonate. In a process similar to the growth of coral reefs which build upon their skeletal remains, stromatolites regrew upon the calcified crust, forming a layered mound. It is the calcium remains and not the plants, which have left a fossil record. Their presence in the limestone layers resemble cabbage heads, and they are exposed along the Going-to-the-Sun Road above the 'loop.'

Dendrites, another type of 'fossil' found in Waterton-Glacier is not a fossil at all. They have a branching figure resembling a miniature tree, shrub, or fern. They are produced in rock fractures by the crystallization of minerals, chiefly oxides of iron and manganese. Occasionally they produce three-dimensional forms. The famous Montana moss-agates are examples of dendrite growth. But most dendrite growth in Waterton-Glacier are two-dimensional forms in the greenish-gray Appekunny Formation and red mudstones of the Grinnell Formation.

The sedimentary layers which were deposited between one billion to 600 million years ago are distinctive and perfectly preserved. It is rare for such ancient rocks exposed to weathering and erosion to remain. These Precambrian formations are distinguishable and a

An ancient sea leaves its impression in rock. Ripple marks (upper left) in the Grinnell Formation indicate they were formed in shallow water. Another indication of ancient shallow seas are found with the formation of Stromatolites (lower left), a primitive form of colonial algae. They were present in the intertidal zone, forming mounds of layered calcium carbonate rinds which have the appearance of fossilized cabbage heads. Layered sedimentary rock (right) also indicates a marine environment.

layer can be "rediscovered" anywhere within the Parks. Glacial carving and polishing have exposed crosscuts of strata, allowing closer inspection of the geologic past. In these cross sections can be seen five main formations, although there are lesser formations found among these. Most formations are two to three thousand feet thick.

The oldest and lowest layer of sedimentary rock—The *Altyn Formation*—is composed of light tan colored limestone and dolomite crisscrossed with layers of quartz sand. In Canada the oldest layer is called the *Waterton Formation*. Some believe it may have been formed as a beach because of the sand layers and the abundant stromatolites found in this formation.

The *Appekunny Formation* lies on top of the Altyn Formation, and consists of greenish-gray mudstones, or argillite. The exposed bedding planes have ripple marks indicating they were formed in shallow water with an alternating wet and dry environment.

The most prominent layer, because of its red to purplish color, is the *Grinnell Formation*. It was laid down during alternate dry and wet environments with bedding planes of ripple marks, mudcracks, and rain drop patterns forming when the mud was soft. This layer is also composed of mudstone, or argillite, with thin layers of green mudstone and white sandstone.

The *Siyeh Formation*, also called the Helena Formation, is primarily composed of dolomite with limestone. This formation weathers slowly and produces ridges and other formations. Organic matter was trapped in the rock when it was formed, and a freshly exposed portion is nearly black in color. As it weathers it turns to shades of tan and light gray. This formation also has abundant stromatolites, indicating it was deposited in very shallow water.

The youngest and highest formations are the *Shepard* and *Kintla Formations*. These formations are rare since they have been eroded by glaciers and water, and only the higher peaks have remaining layers. The Shepard and Kintla formations were also deposited during an alternating wet and dry environment. Weathered tan dolomite, argillite, and siltstones make up the Shepard Formation, while red mudstones form the Kintla Formation.

After the deposition of the Precambrian sedimentary layers molten magma worked its way through the layers forming sills and dikes. The Purcell sill, an igneous intrusion between sedimentary layers, was formed in the upper part of the Siyeh Limestone. This one hundred-foot sill of black diabase is bordered by a zone of white. The organic matter in the limestone was driven out by heat when the molten magma was injected forming the white border. The formation resembles a ribbon along a mountain side.

A dike is formed when an igneous intrusion forms perpendicular to the strata. Diabase weathers fasters than the surrounding country rock, limestone, and a dike or sill forms a groove in the mountain. A diabase dike is exposed along the Going-to-the-Sun Road by the west tunnel. Because of the igneous intrusion of sills and dikes into limestone they often become ore-bearing veins.

Diabase and basalt originally have the same composition, but because of different cooling rates their structure changes. Diabase is the intrusive form which cools slowly, allowing crystallization. Basalt is extrusive, forming basalt flows. It cools quickly resulting in a fine textured rock. Occasionally molten magma reached the surface and flowed as basalt. A basalt flow was incorrectly called granite at the turn-of-the-century, and Granite Park earned its moniker because of that misconception.

More sediments were again deposited during the Paleozoic and Mesozoic eras between 600 and 70 million years ago. Several shallow, inland seas inundated this region depositing

Water polished pebbles have washed ashore on Lake McDonald. The pebbles have been carried by glaciers and streams, and all of the major formations are represented along the shore.

more limestone, mudstones, and sandstones. The Mesozoic Era left marine fossils and oil-bearing sandstone layers. Even though these Paleozoic and Mesozoic layers are not well exposed within the Parks they are an important element in the unusual geologic formation which occurred after their deposition.

The quiet years of the Precambrian to Mesozoic seas ended 65 million years ago when stresses deep within the earth caused continental plates to shift. One hundred miles west of Waterton-Glacier sedimentary layers over the Rocky Mountains began arching. While the sedimentary crust was thrust up several thousand feet, erosion began stripping the younger sediments from the arch. Eventually the incline of the arch became too steep and a thick slab of older Precambrian rock began to slide eastward over younger Mesozoic rock. The sliding began nearly 60 million years ago and ended 10 million years later after a movement of nearly 30 miles. The sliding surface is called the Lewis Overthrust Fault.

As the slab moved it was broken by gaps, one of which is the lower North Fork Valley. Other sections of the slab became isolated by the movement and erosion. Chief Mountain is an isolated slab of Precambrian rock. Outside of the Waterton-Glacier area the slab moved

Grinnell and Sperry glaciers are small examples of the massive glaciers which once occupied the valleys of Waterton-Glacier. During the past three million years four major ice ages came and left this region. Each succeeding ice age destroyed evidence of earlier glaciers, and the present landscape was formed during the last ice age of the Pleistocene Epoch which ended over 10,000 years ago. The massive glaciers during that time filled the valleys completely with glacial ice carving and sculpting valleys like McDonald Valley. Glacier Park was not named for glaciers which now exist, but for its glacial remains.

differently, forming layers like a fallen loaf of sliced bread.

It has taken nearly one billion years to create the Waterton-Glacier landscape. The sediments of Precambrian, and Paleozoic, and Mesozoic seas have formed the foundation for this landscape. The Lewis Overthrust Fault created an unusual phenomena when a slab of Precambrian rock slid on top of younger Mesozoic sediments. And the carving by Pleistocene glaciers have added their finishing touches.

But, like mountain weather, the geology has created an environment which works in harmony. Winter snow and glaciers melt with the coming of summer. Some water plunges over the lip of glaciated hanging canyons, while the remainder trickles into the soil and follows an impervious underground sedimentary layer, only to emerge again as a weeping wall. This is today's geology. It is the movement of water; erosion in action.

ROMANCING
THE MOUNTAINS

The names themselves echo from a romantic period. Names like Lake Josephine, Grinnell Glacier, Cattle Queen Creek, Fusillade Mountain, Mount Blakiston, Never Laughs Mountain, Pitamakan Pass, Vimy Ridge, Garden Wall, and Bird Woman Falls.

A romantic period when Model T's met flappers, with the Clara Bow look of short, navy-blue pongee dresses topped with helmet hats, and men who wore patent leather shoes and sported bowlers upon their heads. And the Blackfeet Indians, dressed in their formal garb, were there too, to greet them as they stepped off the trian at Midvale (now called East Glacier Park).

Model T's and White coaches (open topped busses built by the White Motor Company— forerunner of today's Jammers) carried visitors and their luggage through axle-deep mud, or during dry years through suffocating dust, 52 miles to Many Glacier Hotel. They would arrive there in time for dinner, greeted at the door by bellhops dressed in Swiss-style, suspendered lederhosen who shuttled their luggage to distant rooms. After being served a

The Blackfeet Indians inhabited the prairie east of Waterton-Glacier, subsisting on a staple of buffalo and blue camas bulbs.

hearty dinner the guests and staff gathered in the lobby under silk lanterns around an open fireplace singing, "Five Foot Two, Eyes of Blue, Has Anybody Seen My Girl," "Tea for Two" and "Bye, Bye Blackbird." From there they descended the spiral, stone staircase, set with ferns and a fountain, to a dance hall below the lobby where they would dance the "Charleston" to a brass band until midnight.

At seven o'clock the morning bell would ring and guests arose, men donning tweed knickers and Scottish caps, the women wearing baggy trousers and cloche hats. The wranglers would have the horses groomed, saddled and packed with trail lunches alongside Swiftcurrent Lake by the time guests finished their breakfast. The guide, shy and speechless, would lead the group along the shore, past the remains of an abandoned and unsightly sawmill, and through subalpine firs past Lake Josephine and Grinnell Lake while horseflies buzzed and bit. Horseflies would continue pestering until the guests had gained higher elevation. There the air thinned and a cool breeze blew.

The horse trail ended at a boulder field abutted by a vertical cliff. There the visitors dismounted, hitched the horses to a rail in a small alpine meadow and climbed the remaining distance to Grinnell Glacier. Once they

reached the lateral moraine of Grinnell Glacier the group would stand in awe and unpack ice axes and gold braided rope recently purchased from Abercrombie and Fitch outfitters in New York. They would traverse and cut steps in the glacial ice, anchoring each other as they crossed crevasses. And as the day's outing climaxed the group photographer would pose them for a portrait and snap a shot with his Brownie camera.

The romantic period of the 1920's culminated an era of discovery, exploration, development and politics. The 1920's are still frozen in time. White coaches still meet guests at the East Glacier Park depot, but today the road to Many Glacier is paved and the trip takes less than two hours. Bellhops, still dressed in Swiss attire, greet visitors as they arrive at Many Glacier Hotel, which remains unchanged except for the removal of the stone, spiral staircase. The group singing continues too, even though the songs are from modern musicals. And, whether traveling by horse or foot, the approach route to Grinnell Glacier remains the same.

But most importantly the landscape itself remains unchanged. A hike along a trail takes one back through time, past the 1920's, to when the valleys echoed of trappers, surveyors and prospectors. A glacier itself is a reminder when human history spans nearly 10,000 to 12,000 years ago to the decline of the ice age.

During those cold and changing ice-age days the first inhabitants, living thousands of miles from their ancestral Asian origins, established themselves in this region. The names and even the lifestyles of the first people will always remain a mystery. But their livelihood came from the plains and not from the mountains. Buffalo, or bison, bitterroots and blue camas, all found on the plains east of Glacier, provided them subsistence. Waterton, St. Mary and Two Medicine lakes drew these early people close to the mountains to fish, but their life was essentially devoted to the plains.

Evidence of these first visitors has been found near Waterton Lakes. The discovery of fishing sites along the shores of Waterton Lakes, the finds of crude pottery dating back to 300 A.D. and other finds, indicate this area is rich in archaeology—perhaps one of the richest in the northern Rockies.

The introduction of the horse, about 1700 by the Spanish conquistadores, changed the lifestyle of these American Indians. The horse, introduced to the Blackfeet by the southern Shoshone Indians, provided a more mobile existence. It was during this period that other influences changed their lives, and during this period we also began to know more about the life of these people.

The westward expansion of North American settlers created stress among the tribes as some were forced west into territory already occupied by others. Warfare broke out among Indian tribes which had never crossed paths before. The Blackfeet (who may have been named because of the ash they walked in after a prairie fire) became the prominent tribe to inhabit the plains east of the Parks by the early 1800's. The Kutenai, Kalispel and Flathead (now collectively called the Salish Confederacy) occupied the mountainous region west of the Continental Divide. The only known tribe

to inhabit Waterton-Glacier were the Stoney Indians, a member of the Assiniboines of the plains northeast of Waterton. All of these Indians warred with the Blackfeet, and skirmishes were common.

By the late 18th century the first Europeans began penetrating the Missouri River headwaters country and the Hudson's Bay drainage. Many of these men were French-Canadian trappers under the employment of the Hudson's Bay Company. The Company controlled a vast territory "defined as all lands watered by streams flowing into Hudson's Bay," which extended from the Bay to Triple Divide Peak. Most of these trappers left no record of their journeys, and many never returned to tell of their accounts. Whoever first discovered, or sighted, the Waterton-Glacier country may remain unnamed. However, one of the first recorded accounts of this country comes from David Thompson, British explorer for the Hudson's Bay Company, who made a reconnaissance to the area north of Waterton Park in November 1787. He stated in his journal: "At length the Rocky Mountains came in sight like shining white clouds in the horizon, but we doubted what our guide said; but as we proceeded, they rose in height their immense masses of snow appeared above the clouds, and formed an impassable barrier, even to the Eagle."

The Americans took an official interest in this region after the Louisiana Territory was purchased from France in 1803. President Thomas Jefferson sent the Lewis and Clark Expedition to explore the upper Missouri River, to find a possible route to the Pacific Ocean and to document their findings. On their return journey the Expedition divided. Lewis and his party left the Bitterroot Valley, south of Glacier, to travel to the "Great Falls of the Missouri" and explored the headwaters of the Marias River. The object was to determine if the Missouri River drainage extended past the 49th parallel.

When Lewis reached his farthest point north, between Cutbank and Browning, on July 22, 1806 the mountains of Glacier loomed 25 miles away when he wrote in his journal: *"...the plain on which we are is very high; the rocky mountains to the S.W. of us appear but low from their base yet are partially covered with snow nearly to their bases, there is no timber on those mountains within our view; they are very irregular and broken in their form and seem to be composed principally of clay with but little rock or stone..."*

The activity around Waterton-Glacier flourished briefly during the beginning of the 19th century. Most of this activity was undertaken by trappers of the Hudson's Bay Company, who were under the leadership of David Thompson.

Hudson's Bay Company agent Peter Fidler traveled along the eastern base of the mountains, and he was the first to place a name to this region. A British map later published 'King's Mountain,' now called Chief Mountain, as the prominent landmark for this region.

Thomspon also began establishing trading posts west of the Continental Divide, avoiding hostile Blackfeet country on the plains. One of Thompson's employees, Finian MacDonald, while passing through the mountains to hunt bison on the plains, became the first recorded European to enter the area now known as Glacier Park.

From the early to mid 1800's activity in the Rocky Mountains dwindled. The fur industry collapsed by the late 1830's and the Blackfeet restricted most travel within their territory. Only the Catholic and Protestant missionaries ventured into the territory during this period. Belgian Jesuit, Pierre-Jean de Smet was the most famous of these. He traveled extensively through the Rocky Mountains and established St. Mary's Mission in the Bitterroot Valley in 1841 for the Flatheads. Later, in 1854, St. Ignatius Mission was established by the Jesuits in the Flathead Valley for the Kalispels. But their attempt to convert the Blackfeet to Christianity hurt their work with the Flatheads and Kalis-pels and as a result they were unable to make progress for the next 20 years.

By the mid 1800's Waterton-Glacier again became the center of activity as territory ownership was disputed. The Louisiana Purchase left doubt as to the actual northern boundary of the United States, and different foreign claims were also in conflict. An agreement was made in 1818 to delineate the 49th parallel from Lake of the Woods in Minnesota to the Continental Divide. However, west of the Continental Divide the issue became contested when the valuable Columbia River drainage was at stake. The Oregon settlers began advancing into British territory, and they were unwilling to give up prime agricultural land. "Fifty-four forty or fight" became the cry to establish the American boundary. The Hudson's Bay Company had held claim to this region, but with the decline of the fur industry and the lack of defense for this territory the British government offered a compromise. In 1846 President James Polk accepted the British offer and extended the Lake of the Woods-Continental Divide boundary along the 49th parallel.

A new era was emerging after the 1850's. The industrial revolution in the New England states was affecting the entire country. The push for transcontinental railroads became a public obsession, and the need to organize land into homestead parcels became an objective for surveyors.

Since Lewis and Clark's time there had been a desire to find a low passage through the Rocky Mountains. Lewis and Clark had difficulty, and nearly lost their lives, when crossing Lolo Pass during their journey to the Pacific. On

The romantic period of the 1920's brought a new era to Waterton-Glacier. The Great Northern Railroad began bringing eastern 'dudes' to explore the backcountry glaciers, like Blackfoot Glacier.

their return trip they sighted, without knowing, the lowest and easiest passage through the mountains at Marias Pass.

The construction of a transcontinental railroad was a monumental task, and the government appointed Issac Stevens, Governor of Washington Territory, to survey the Pacific Northwest and, in particular, to find a suitable passage for a railroad. Stevens sent engineers with Indian guides to the Flathead Valley to report on the rumored Marias Pass, described to him by the Blackfeet Chief Little Dog. A.W. Tinkham explored the east slope of the mountains during 1853 and reported that Marias Pass (he was actually at Pitamakan Pass to the north) was unsuitable for a railroad without the construction of a tunnel. Stevens was disappointed with this report and in the following year he sent John Doty to explore further. Doty described Tinkham's find and verified his report. However, when he traveled farther south he sighted the true Marias Pass. Doty was unable to investigate thoroughly, but he stated that this was the Marias Pass described by Little Dog.

The discovery of Marias Pass meant an easy route for a northern railroad was possible. The nearest passage through the Rockies was Rogers Pass to the south, 100 miles away, and Crowsnest Pass 150 miles to the north in Canada. Even though this discovery was not acted upon for over 30 years it became one of the most important discoveries for the railroad.

The Civil War years distracted interest in the northern Rockies until 1889 when Marias Pass was 'rediscovered.' James Hill, owner of the Great Northern Railroad, sent engineer John Stevens (no relation to Issac Stevens) to Marias Pass to mark a practical route for his westward expanding railroad. Stevens confirmed the pass as a feasible crossing for the railroad, and became the new 'discoverer' of Marias Pass.

By the spring of 1890 survey crews had staked a route through the mountains to the Flathead Valley. By the following year the railroad was completed to Kalispell, and the entire track to the Pacific was finished in less than two years. The entire territory was then open to development.

Prior to the completion of the railraod the first scientific survey of the northern Rockies was lead by John Palliser. A member of his expedition, Thomas Blakiston, lead a group to the Waterton Park area and became the first to name and record the features there. He named the international lake Waterton in honor of the English naturalist, Squire Charles Waterton. This expedition was also the first of many scientific surveys to mark the international boundary between Waterton and Glacier.

During Blakiston's visit to Waterton, Issac Stevens had begun negotiating peace among the Salish tribes and established a reservation, extending east of the Continental Divide. Nevertheless Blackfeet-settler skirmishes continued through the 1870's. And by the 1890's a mad rush to find gold in the mountains caused the government to buy back the strip of land along the east slope of the Continental Divide which is now the eastern half of Glacier Park.

Gold rush fever brought another era to Waterton-Glacier. Prospectors who had left the gold fields of Bannack, Alder Gulch, and Last Chance Gulch began looking north for more gold. By 1884 gold-bearing ore was discovered in the mountains of the Blackfeet Indian Reservation. By 1889 news of the profitable "Dutch Lui" strike had spread. Prospectors began roaming through the mountains west of the Continental Divide, and they began seeking greener pastures on the east slope of the Divide in the Blackfeet Reservation. By 1898 the Blackfeet, knowing they had no choice, sold the land east of the Continental Divide for $1.5 million.

The opening of the east slope brought a gold rush to the mountains. Nearly 2,000 claims were staked within what is now the Park, and a boom town began growing in the Swiftcurrent Valley. Altyn (near the present site of Many

Glacier) soon had a population of nearly 1,000, a newspaper, post office, and a hotel. The gold rush, however, did not last long. The gold and copper finds were meager, the work was hard, and most prospectors soon began leaving for the Klondike.

Precious metals were not the only discoveries in the area. By 1902 oil was found seeping from the ground in Cameron Valley. It was the first oil find in western Canada. An oil well was drilled and Oil City developed on the site. More oil drilling at Kintla Lake and Swiftcurrent Valley followed. But oil, like gold, proved to be meager and all oil developments were soon abandoned.

By the turn-of-the-century another discovery proved to be the most valuable of all—the mountains themselves. Homesteaders were attracted to the valleys and lakes. Even though the winters were harsh and a living was hard to make they found solitude and the romance of the mountains ample reward.

The arrival of the Great Northern Railroad and the popularity of the mountains prompted James Hill, creator of the Great Northern Railroad, to establish a series of hotels and backcountry chalets. The Many Glacier Hotel (left), completed in 1915, is the largest hotel in the Parks. Even though most of the backcountry chalets were abandoned and torn down during World War II, Sperry (above) and Granite Park chalets are still reminders of the "Empire Building" railroad.

James Hill's "Empire Building" railroad through Marias Pass helped bring Waterton-Glacier into the 20th century. The railroad stations at Belton (now called West Glacier) and Midvale (now called East Glacier Park) began leaving curious visitors who would hike the two miles to sit along the pebble shore of Lake McDonald or silently gaze at the mountains while waiting a layover at the station. Others, like Dr. Lyman Sperry or George Bird Grinnell, left the railroad depot to explore the natural history hidden among the mountains. Sperry, a geologist, found evidence of glacial carving in the McDonald Valley, and his insight lead to the discovery of several active glaciers. He later helped to promote tourism in Glacier and protested against wanton development. Grinnell, publisher and editor of *Forest and Stream* magazine, also traversed and explored the mountains, returning home to write about his adventures. Grinnell and others began suggesting Glacier should be protected. Waterton had already received some protection when it was initially established as Kootenay Lake Forest Reserve in 1895.

A national park group began gaining momentum by 1907, and a National Park Bill was introduced by Montana Senator Thomas Carter in that year. The bill failed in its first year, but it was reintroduced annually until it was finally passed and signed into law May 11, 1910 by President William Taft.

The following year Waterton also became a national park with the help of "Kootenai Brown," local resident and game warden. Waterton also had political problems, the Forest Reserve when declared a national park was reduced from 54 square miles to only a fourth of that amount, and this reduction did

A relic of the past. The International Boat, on its maiden voyage (left) is christened by its builders and crew. The wooden ship is still navigated from the original pilot house (right) as it plies the international waters of Waterton Lake.

not cover most of the shoreline of Waterton Lakes. However it was enlarged in 1941 to its present size of 423 square miles. The uniqueness of the two countries sharing a mountain range, a lake, a national park and peace prompted Alberta and Montana Rotarians in 1932 to seek legislation to declare these two as Waterton-Glacier International Peace Park.

The development of the railroad and the establishment of two national parks opened the door to tourism and development. James Hill saw the need for visitor accommodations. By 1910 the Great Northern Railroad began construction on Belton Chalet, followed by Glacier Park Lodge, Many Glacier Hotel, Two Medicine, Goat Haunt, Cut Bank, Gunsight, St. Mary, Sperry and Granite Park chalets, Lake McDonald Lodge and Prince of Wales Hotel. Temporary tent camps were also established in more remote regions of the Parks. Each major lake had passenger boats plying the cold waters throughout the summer. The major hotels provided horse rides or coach transportation between the hotels and chalets. All of this development was completed in less than 20 years—a major accomplishment.

There was also a need for roads into the Park. Even though the rugged topography was an obstacle to the construction of roads, one was envisioned in 1910 by Glacier Park's first superintendent. By 1933 the Going-to-the-Sun Road had been built and was open. The completion of the 50 mile, $3 million road, which required the blasting of and removal of millions of tons of rock, and excavation of two tunnels during the short alpine summers was another major accomplishment.

Other developments threatened Waterton-Glacier's existence. In the early 1920's the Canadian government proposed building a dam at the outlet of Waterton Lake. It would have raised the lake level 40 feet. The proposal was defeated, as was the 1950's proposal for the Glacier View Dam in the North Fork Valley. That project would have flooded 25 miles of the valley. Despite those victories other dams were constructed. Lake Sherburne, a fluctuating reservoir, inundated the town of Altyn and the site of the first oil well. And the Lower Two Medicine reservoir is now rendered useless by the accumulation of sediments.

There will always be a struggle to maintain a pristine environment in a national park. Outside developments will nibble at its border, but inside its border the romance of the mountains will always remain.

BIBLIOGRAPHY

HIKING

Nelson, Dick and Sharon. 1978. *Hikers Guide to Glacier National Park.* Glenwood, New Mexico: Tecolote Press, Inc.

Sumner, David and Danny On. 1979. *Along the Trail.* West Glacier: Glacier Natural History Association.

NATURE

Beaumont, Greg. 1978. *Many-Storied Mountains.* Washington D.C.: U.S. Government Printing Office.

Shaw, Richard J. and Danny On. 1979. *Plants of Waterton-Glacier National Park.* Missoula, Montana: Mountain Press Publishing Co.

GEOLOGY

Alt, David D. and Donald W. Hyndman. 1973. *Rocks, Ice and Water.* Missoula, Montana: Mountain Press Publishing Co.

Raup, Omer B., et al. 1983. *Geology Along Going-to-the-Sun Road.* West Glacier: Glacier NHA.

HISTORY

Bucholtz, C.W. 1975. *Man in Glacier.* West Glacier: Glacier NHA

Thompson, David and Victor G. Hopwood, editor. 1971. *David Thompson: Travels in Western North American, 1784-1812.* Toronto, Canada: Macmillian.

Williams, M.B. 1982(reprint). *Waterton Lakes National Park.* Lethbridge, Alberta: Historic Trails Society of Alberta.

FOR MORE PARK INFORMATION WRITE:

WATERTON

    Park Superintendent
    Waterton Lakes National Park
    Waterton Park, Alberta, T0K 2M0 Canada

GLACIER

    Superintendent, Glacier National Park
    West Glacier, Montana 59936 U.S.A.

SERVICES

WATERTON

CRANDALL MOUNTAIN · campground, firewood.

WATERTON TOWNSITE · campground, (hook-ups available), visitor center, warden office, medical, accomodations, service stations, restaurants, snack bars, groceries, bar and lounges, bank, gift shops, horse rides, boat cruises, rentals and launch, bicycle rentals, golf, laundry, showers, post office.

CAMERON LAKE · boat and fishing rentals.

BELLY RIVER · campground, firewood.

SERVICES

GLACIER

GOAT HAUNT (accessible by foot or boat only) · camping shelter, ranger station, boat dock.

POLEBRIDGE · campgrounds (Kintla Lake, Mud Creek, River, Bowman Lake, and Creek, Quartz Creek, and Logging Creek), ranger station, groceries, gifts, post office.

MANY GLACIER · campground (hard-sided vehicles only), ranger station, accomodations, service station, restaurants, snack bar, groceries, bar and lounge, gift shops, horse rides, boat cruise and rentals, firewood.

ST. MARY · campground, visitor centers, ranger station, cabins, service stations, restaurants, snack bar, groceries, bar and lounge, gift shops, laundry, post office.

RISING SUN · campground, accomodations, service station, restaurant, groceries, gift shops, boat cruise, showers, firewood.

LOGAN PASS · visitor center.

GRANITE PARK CHALET (accessible by foot or horse only) backcountry campground, accomodations, food service.

AVALANCHE CREEK · campground (hard-sided vehicles only), ranger station.

LAKE MCDONALD LODGE · accommodations, service station, restaurants, snack bar, groceries, bar and lounge, gift shops, horse rides, boat cruise and rentals, post office, firewood.

SPERRY CHALET (accessible by foot or horse only) · accomodations, food service.

SPRAGUE CREEK · campground (tents only).

FISH CREEK · campground.

APGAR · campground, visitor center, ranger station, Park headquarters, accomodations, gas, restaurant, groceries, bar and lounge, gift shops, horse rides, boat rentals and launch, bicycle rentals, golf, laundry, firewood.

WEST GLACIER/BELTON · medical, motels, service stations, train station, restaurants, groceries, bar and lounge, gift shops, laundry, post office.

CUTBANK · campground.

TWO MEDICINE · campground, ranger station, gas, snack bar, groceries, gift shop, boat cruise, rentals and launch, firewood.

EAST GLACIER · accomodations, service stations, train station, restaurant, snack bar, groceries, bar and lounges, gift shops, laundry, post office.

WALTON · ranger station.

BOOKS IN THIS SERIES

Grand Teton	Death Valley
Yellowstone	Glacier-Waterton